OKLAHOMA DRUG LAWS

Offenses, Penalties, & Your Rights

Frank A. Urbanic, Esq.

ISBN: 978-1-946481-05-4

Designed and Published by:

Speakeasy Publications
73-03 Bell Blvd, #10
Oakland Gardens, NY 11364
www.SpeakeasyMarketingInc.com
888-225-8594

DISCLAIMER

This publication is intended to be informational only. No legal advice is being given, and no attorney-client relationship is intended to be created by reading this material. If you are facing legal issues, whether criminal or civil, seek professional legal counsel to get your questions answered. The law cited is current as of May 1, 2017. Laws are subject to change at any time.

THE URBANIC LAW FIRM, PLLC
1141 N Robinson Avenue
Suite 101
Oklahoma City, OK 73103
(405) 633-3420

Frank@Urbanic.Law

www.Urbanic.Law

TABLE OF CONTENTS

About Frank Urbanic

I became a criminal defense attorney because I'm intimately familiar with how precious our constitutional rights are. After my arrest years ago, I realized how close I was to being in a situation that could have negatively impacted my life forever. That experience made me realize how important it is to have someone on your side who feels strongly about protecting your rights.

In the Air Force, I put my life on the line to support and defend the Constitution during combat. Today, I support and defend the Constitution in the courtroom. My legal career began by representing indigent clients. I saw first-hand how important it is for everyone to have legal representation.

Through my extensive business training at The University of Oklahoma and elsewhere, I've learned proven business techniques that allow me to operate a lean and efficient law firm. These techniques include document automation, checklists, templates, the use of cutting-edge technology, and continuous process improvement practices. My firm uses these business techniques to produce high-quality legal representation in a fraction of the time. Less waste means more value to my clients.

While many offices are still dealing with paper folders, we are digital. No missing documents. No messy folders. Using cloud-based technology, I can work on your case from anywhere on the planet. Whether I'm in a Starbucks or in an airplane at 30,000 ft, I'm still able to work on cases.

What Makes My Firm Particularly Suited To Helping You With Defending Your Rights?

- Extensive Experience In Handling Criminal Defense Cases
- Rated Superb On AVVO.com
- Employing Cutting-Edge Technology To The Benefit Of Our Clients
- Providing High-Quality Criminal Defense At A Reasonable Price

- Intensive Criminal Defense Training In The Caprock Regional Public Defender Office

My Firm Has Handled Cases In The Following Areas:

- Criminal Defense
- DUI, DWI, & APC
- Domestic Assault & Battery
- Theft Crimes
- Drug Possession, Distribution, and Trafficking
- Traffic Tickets

Additional Training:

- Standard Field Sobriety Test Instructor
- Standard Field Sobriety Test Practitioner
- Advanced Roadside Impaired Driving Enforcement Practitioner
- Drug Recognition Expert Overview course graduate

Professional Associations And Memberships

- National Association of Criminal Defense Lawyers
- National College for DUI Defense
- Oklahoma Criminal Defense Lawyers Association

- Oklahoma Bar Association
- Oklahoma County Bar Association
- Canadian County Bar Association
- Oklahoma County Criminal Defense Lawyers Association
- Order of the Coif
- Phi Kappa Phi

Bar Admissions

- Oklahoma

Overview Of Oklahoma's Criminal Process

This section outlines the criminal process in an Oklahoma county court. Municipalities only charge people with misdemeanors. The municipal court process is generally more abbreviated than a county court's process.

Investigation

After a crime is allegedly committed, law enforcement will investigate the allegations. The investigation may include interviewing the victim, witnesses, & suspects; collecting physical evidence; visiting, photographing, & examining evidence at the crime scene; and identifying suspects.

Arrest

When a crime is committed in a law enforcement officer's presence or the officer has probable cause to believe that certain misdemeanors or any felony was committed out of the officer's presence, an officer may arrest a suspect on the spot without an arrest warrant. An arrest may not occur immediately after a crime is reported because the law enforcement officer may need to conduct further investigation. In either case, the officer will then submit a Probable Cause Affidavit to the District Attorney, suggesting potential charges to be authorized.

Next, the prosecutor determines whether a person should be charged with a crime and, if so, what the crime should be. The prosecutor must thoroughly review all reports and records concerning the case, including witness statements. The prosecutor also reviews the suspect's criminal record. Occasionally, the reviewing prosecutor sends the case back to the police to conduct additional investigation.

The prosecutor can issue a charge if he or she reasonably believes that probable cause exists that the suspect committed the offense. However, prosecutors should apply a higher standard—whether the charge can be proved beyond a reasonable doubt at trial with the information known at that time. A

warrant for arrest will be issued when the prosecutor issues the charges.

Arrest occurs when the police officer takes the suspect into jail. Booking is the process of actually putting the suspect in jail.

Initial Court Appearance - Arraignment

This is the first time a defendant will go before a judge. The defendant's legal rights will be described, an initial plea of not guilty will be entered, and a bond will be set. In some cases, this bond may be an "Own Recognizance Bond" (OR bond), which requires no payment of money to a bondsman. The judge will tell the defendant when to appear in court next. The next court date will typically be about a month out. The defendant will receive a copy of the Information and Probable Cause Affidavit. The Information briefly describes what the defendant did to violate the law and cites the statute the defendant allegedly violated. The Probable Cause Affidavit is like a mini police report.

All further pre-trial procedures are determined by whether the defendant is charged with a felony or misdemeanor.

Misdemeanor

The defendant will typically be placed on a disposition docket. While on the disposition docket, the defendant must decide whether to plead guilty (or no contest) or go to trial. The defendant's attorney will use the time the defendant is on the disposition docket to gather evidence, investigate, and negotiate with the prosecutor. The trial procedures listed below are mostly the same for felonies and misdemeanors. A major difference between the misdemeanor and felony procedures is that the defendant does not get the opportunity for a preliminary hearing in a misdemeanor case.

Felony

Preliminary Hearing Conference (PHC)

These appearances are a time for the attorney and the prosecutor to discuss the case. The prosecutor will make a plea bargain recommendation. The attorney will negotiate with the prosecutor to try and improve the negotiated plea. If the defendant accepts the offer, he or she would waive—or give up—their right to a trial and plead guilty. If the defendant does not accept the plea recommendation, the case will be set for a preliminary hearing.

Preliminary Hearing

A preliminary hearing is a court hearing where witnesses testify and a judge decides whether there is enough evidence against the defendant to order a trial. The State must present enough evidence to show the court probable cause that a crime was committed and probable cause that the defendant committed the crime. The defendant will be "bound over" for trial if the court believes the State presented enough evidence to show there is probable cause to believe the defendant committed the crime(s). Probable cause is a very low standard. The vast majority of defendants get bound over. The prosecutor is not required to present all of their witnesses or all of the evidence they have collected. They are only required to present enough evidence to meet the probable cause standard. The defendant, through his or her attorney, can cross-examine the witnesses and may have the opportunity to present evidence—including witnesses.

If the judge decides that there is not probable cause that the defendant committed the charged crime(s), the judge can bind the case over on different charges, reduce the charges to misdemeanors for trial in District Court, or dismiss charges. A defendant can give up his or her right to a preliminary hearing by waiving it. Many prosecutors will threaten to make the plea recommendation worse if a preliminary hearing occurs. A preliminary hearing should generally be conducted if there is a strong belief that the case will go to trial. The preliminary hearing gives the defense an opportunity to see some of the State's evidence, gather information for further investigation, and get witness testimony on the record.

Pre-Trial Conference (PTC)

If a defendant loses the preliminary hearing, he or she will appear before a judge to get arraigned. The defendant will enter a plea of not guilty and receive the official charging documents. After the arraignment or waiver of preliminary hearing, the defendant will be on the PTC docket. This gives the attorney additional time to negotiate and investigate. A defendant may still plead during this phase; they are not required to go to trial.

The defense is not entitled to receive certain evidence until various points in time, so prosecutors often withhold evidence until they are required by law to turn it over. Generally, prosecutors will keep evidence such as video, audio, pictures, and medical reports away from the defense as long as possible. Prosecutors typically begin turning over more evidence once the case is set for trial.

Pre-Trial Hearing

The trial court judge may be called upon to resolve various pre-trial issues. Some will determine whether the case will continue to a trial, be resolved with a plea, or be dismissed. Various motions may be heard that can affect what evidence will be admissible at trial. These include a motion for discovery, motion in limine, motion to suppress, and motion to dismiss.

Jury Call Docket

This is a hearing where the defendant and his or her attorney meet with the judge and the prosecutor to announce whether the defendant wants to go to trial or plead guilty. If the defendant decides to proceed to trial, the judge will schedule the trial's start date.

Trial

Either a judge or jury may determine guilt. A bench trial is where a jury is waived and the judge alone decides whether the defendant is guilty or not guilty. In most cases, both sides must agree to waive a jury and proceed to a bench trial. For the State to win a trial, the prosecutor must present enough evidence to prove beyond a reasonable doubt that the defendant committed the crime(s) he or she is accused of committing.

A jury trial starts by the random selection of local county residents from a list of licensed drivers. They are summoned to the court as potential jurors. The judge, prosecutor, and defense attorney question the jurors about their backgrounds and beliefs. This is called "voir dire." The attorneys are permitted to kick off a limited number potential jurors.

After twelve (or six for misdemeanor trials) acceptable jurors remain, the judge administers an oath to the jury and reads basic instructions. The prosecutor gives an opening statement to outline the State's case and evidence to the jury. The defense may give an opening statement or wait until later in the trial. The prosecutor calls witnesses, which the defense may cross examine. After presenting all the State's evidence, the State will rest its case. If the judge determines at that time that there is not enough evidence that a jury would find the defendant guilty, then the judge will dismiss the case.

If there is enough evidence that a jury might find the defendant guilty, then the defendant will have an opportunity to present evidence. There is no requirement for the defendant to present evidence. The defense may call witnesses, and the prosecutor may cross-examine them. The defense rests after they have presented their case. The prosecutor may present rebuttal witnesses and evidence to challenge evidence presented by the defendant, and the State will rest upon conclusion of their rebuttal. Occasionally, the trial judge will let the defense present a surrebuttal case to respond to the State's rebuttal witnesses' testimony.

The prosecutor presents their closing argument to the jury first. Next, the defense presents its closing argument to the jury. Since the State has the burden of proof, the prosecutor may present the final closing argument to rebut the defendant. The judge gives the jury instructions about the charged crimes and the deliberation process. Finally, the jury retires to the jury room and deliberates.

To convict, the jury must determine guilt beyond a reasonable doubt. If the jurors have a reasonable doubt as to guilt, then the jury must find the defendant not guilty. The only way the jury may convict the accused is for all members to find evidence of guilt beyond a reasonable doubt.

If all members of the jury find the defendant not guilty, the case is over. If the jury finds the defendant guilty, then the case proceeds to sentencing. If the defendant has a prior felony conviction that will be used to enhance the current sentence, then guilt is decided in one stage and sentencing is decided in another stage. The second stage is a mini trial that is conducted just for purposes of sentencing. A defendant does not have the right to waive jury sentencing or demand sentencing by the judge.

A jury recommends a sentence, and a judge determines the final sentence. A judge must give the sentence returned by the jury, but the judge may be able to deviate from the sentence when allowed by statute or in the public interest. If the defendant is charged with more than one count, the judge may decide whether to run the counts concurrently or consecutively. In most cases, the judge sentences the defendant to what the jury decided.

If the jury does not come to a unanimous decision, the case will be declared a mistrial. If this happens, the State can choose to either retry the case, no longer pursue charges against the defendant, or offer a new plea deal.

Appeal

Every person convicted in Oklahoma is entitled to an appeal of their conviction to the Court of Criminal Appeals. Certain actions must be taken within statutorily prescribed time periods, so time is of the essence when considering an appeal.

Plea Options

Plea negotiations typically end up with the defendant pleading to either a deferred or suspended sentence. Both involve an amount of time on probation. The probation may be supervised or unsupervised. If it is supervised, a defendant must regularly report to a probation officer. If it is unsupervised, a defendant simply must obey the rules of probation and not break the law.

Deferred Sentence

With a deferred sentence, the defendant pleads guilty but does not receive an immediate conviction. The judge finds the defendant guilty of the crime but postpones (or "defers") sentencing until a later date. If the defendant does everything the court orders them to do, the court will dismiss the case and the charge will not appear on the defendant's record. A defendant may be ordered to, for example, pay all court costs and fees, see a probation officer, go to treatment, and not break the law again. If the defendant does not successfully complete the deferred sentence requirements or adhere to the terms of probation, the court may sentence him or her to jail or prison.

Suspended Sentence

With a suspended sentence, the defendant pleads guilty, receives an immediate conviction, and is sentenced to a term in jail or prison. But, all or part of the sentence is suspended and the defendant is put on probation for the period of time that the sentence is suspended. The defendant does not have to go to prison for that amount of time as long as he or she satisfies the conditions of probation. If the defendant violates the terms of probation, he or she may be sentenced to spend the entire sentence in jail or prison.

Dismissal

My goal in every case is dismissal. However, that is not always possible. Dismissal typically requires a strong legal reason or very compelling mitigating circumstances. Prosecutors are very hesitant to dismiss a case. However, they are more likely to dismiss a case if they can be persuaded with some legal reason why they would not succeed if the case were to go to trial. Sometimes, a plea deal can be worked out where one or more counts are dismissed in exchange for a guilty plea on one or more other counts.

Reduce to Misdemeanor

It may be possible to have some cases that were originally filed as a felony reduced to a misdemeanor through plea negotiations. Prosecutors may reduce any non "85% crime" to a misdemeanor. An "85% crime" is one that is considered especially bad, such as murder and rape. They are listed in 21 OS § 13.1 Per 22 OS § 234, any felony not listed in 21 OS § 13.1 can be charged as a misdemeanor.

Blind Plea

A blind plea is essentially where the defendant throws themselves on the mercy of the court. Think of it like a mini trial. The defendant admits guilt and basically asks the judge for mercy. The prosecutor puts on their case as to why the defendant should receive the punishment the prosecutor thinks the defendant deserves. Then, the defense tells the court what they think the punishment should be. As a defense attorney, we hope that the judge sees our point of view better than the prosecutor's.

This is a good time to present mitigating evidence that you may not have been able to bring up in trial, so it's a good idea to know a lot about the client's background and good things they've done. For instance, you can talk about the client's military service and their upbringing. Maybe they lived in a foster home and had a lot of very negative influences, or maybe their parents were drug addicts. These are things that a defense attorney can use to humanize the client and hopefully get the judge to feel sympathy. A blind plea is a good thing to do when the offer from the prosecutor is bad, you don't think that going to a jury trial would get you a much better outcome, and you think the judge would give you a better sentence than either of those two previous options.

SOURCES:

Title 22 of the Oklahoma Statutes – Criminal Procedure
21 OS §13.1
22 OS § 234

RECENT CHANGES TO OKLAHOMA'S DRUG LAWS

Oklahoma has one of the highest incarceration rates in the country. Our prisons and county jails are overflowing, and a significant percentage of the people who are incarcerated or in jail are there for simple possession.

People are generally fed up with the system. They don't like how people who are doing nothing more than using drugs are sometimes put in jail longer than people who harm others. The public is waking up. There is a lot of interest in criminal justice reform these days. I think people want to make sure that we are focusing our resources, both on the prosecution and incarceration side, on people who need to be removed from society.

Where Things Stand With The Changed Drug Laws As Of November 2016

A law that went into effect November 1, 2016 changed the sentencing range for simple possession of drugs. It eliminated the mandatory minimum time and reduced the maximum time for the first offense of simple drug possession. However, a ballot measure passed on November 8, 2016 changed that same law again. The change goes into effect on July 1, 2017. It makes simple possession of any drug a misdemeanor—no matter how many times somebody has been arrested for possession of drugs, what kind of drugs they were caught with, or where they were when they got caught with drugs.

Oklahoma went from one of the harshest states for drug possession to potentially the most lenient state for drug possession. To put this in perspective, the law that was superseded on November 1, 2016 had 899 words. The law in effect from November 1, 2016 to July 1, 2017 has 947 words. The law that goes into effect on July 1, 2017, has only 290 words. It's clear that a lot was removed from the previous laws, most of which involved categorizing different punishments based on the schedules and how many times someone has been convicted of drug possession. The new law also takes out any reference to the possession of drugs in front of children or near schools. No matter where you possess drugs, what kinds of drugs, or how many times you get caught possessing drugs, starting July 1, 2017, it will be considered a misdemeanor.

Some people claim that changing simple possession from a felony to a misdemeanor will prevent people from entering drug court because a felony offense is required to enter drug court. However, 22 OS § 471.1 authorizes the establishment of a drug court for misdemeanor offenses.

SOURCES:

22 OS § 471.1
22 OS § 471.2
63 OS § 2-402 (Superseded 11/1/16)
63 OS § 2-402 (Superseded 7/1/2017)
63 OS § 2-402 (Effective 7/1/2017)

SCHEDULES OF CONTROLLED SUBSTANCES

Oklahoma uses the same drug schedules as the Federal Government—I through V. Oklahoma will use the scheduling system for both possession of drugs and possession with intent to distribute through June 30, 2017. On July 1, 2017, these schedules will only apply to possession with intent to distribute. Assuming the law covering simple possession does not change, the schedule of drugs will not matter for simple possession of any drug because it will always be a misdemeanor.

Schedule I

Schedule I drugs are substances that have a high potential for abuse and no accepted medical use in the United States or lack accepted safety use in treatment under medical supervision. Some of the more well-known Schedule I drugs are heroin, MDMA, ecstasy, psilocybin, GHB, marijuana, PCP, LSD, and synthetic marijuana.

Schedule II

Schedule II drugs are substances with the following characteristics: high potential for abuse; currently accepted medical use in the United States, or currently accepted medical use with severe restrictions; and the abuse of the substance may lead to severe psychic or physical dependence. Schedule II drugs include amphetamine, cocaine, methadone, oxycodone, codeine, hydrocodone, morphine, and methamphetamine.

Schedule III

Schedule III drugs are substances that have the following characteristics: a potential for abuse less than the substances enlisted in Schedules I and II; currently accepted medical use in treatment in the United States; and abuse may lead to moderate or low physical dependence or high psychological dependence. Popular Schedule III drugs include many steroids and ketamine.

Schedule IV

Schedule IV drugs include substances with the following characteristics: low potential for abuse relative to substances listed in Schedule III; currently accepted medical use in treatment in use in the United States; and abuse of the substance may be due to limited physical, or psychological dependence relative to the substances listed in Schedule III. Well-known Schedule IV drugs include benzodiazepines (e.g. Xanax, Valium, and Ativan), Ambien, and Tramadol.

Schedule V

Schedule V includes substances with the following characteristics: low potential for abuse relative to the substances listed in Schedule IV; currently accepted medical use in treatment in the United States; and limited physical dependence or psychological dependence relative to the controlled substances listed in Schedule IV. Schedule V drugs include drugs that are generally compounds or mixtures that contain limited quantities of various drugs including codeine, opium, pseudoephedrine, or ephedrine.

SOURCES:
63 OS § 2-203
63 OS § 2-204

63 OS § 2-205
63 OS § 2-206
63 OS § 2-207
63 OS § 2-208
63 OS § 2-209
63 OS § 2-210
63 OS § 2-211
63 OS § 2-212

DRUG PARAPHERNALIA

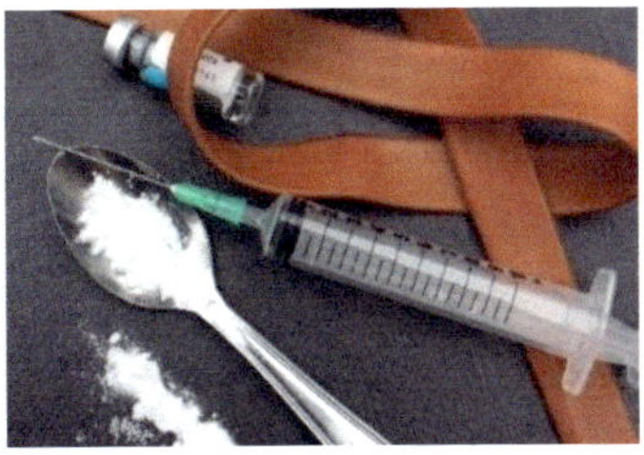

It is a crime to possess drug paraphernalia in Oklahoma. The law prohibiting drug paraphernalia in Oklahoma is 63 OS § 2-405. The factors used to determine what constitutes paraphernalia are listed in 63 OS § 2-101.1. Possession of paraphernalia is a misdemeanor. It is a felony for someone 18 or older to deliver or sell paraphernalia to somebody under 18.

A court will look at the following factors to determine what constitutes "drug paraphernalia":

1. Statements by an owner or by anyone in control of the object concerning its use;
2. The proximity of the object, in time and space, to a direct violation of the Uniform Controlled Dangerous Substances Act;
3. The proximity of the object to controlled dangerous substances;
4. The existence of any residue of controlled dangerous substances on the object;

5. Direct or circumstantial evidence of the intent of an owner, or of anyone in control of the object, to deliver it to any person who intends to use the object to facilitate a violation of the Uniform Controlled Dangerous Substances Act.;
6. Instructions, oral or written, provided with the object which either state directly or imply that the object is to be used for the consumption of controlled substances;
7. Descriptive materials accompanying the object which explain or depict its use as an object for the consumption of controlled substances;
8. The manner in which the object is displayed for sale;
9. Whether the owner, or anyone in control of the object, is a legitimate supplier of like or related items to the community, such as a licensed distributor or dealer of tobacco products;
10. Direct or circumstantial evidence of the ratio of sales of the object or objects to the total sales of the business enterprise;
11. The existence and scope of legitimate uses for the object in the community; and
12. Expert testimony concerning its use.

The innocence of an owner, or of anyone in control of the object, as to a direct violation of this law shall not prevent a finding that the object is intended for use, or fashioned specifically for use, as drug paraphernalia.

SOURCES:
63 OS § 2-101.1
63 OS § 2-405

Possession Of A Controlled Dangerous Substance (CDS)

Possession of a controlled dangerous substance (CDS) in Oklahoma is often referred to as "simple" possession. When someone is charged with simple possession, the belief is that they possessed drugs only for personal use. The person caught with drugs didn't have an intent to distribute nor were they trafficking. The primary statute covering possession of drugs in Oklahoma is 63 OS § 2-402.

Section 2-402 changed on November 1, 2016, and it changes again on July 1, 2017. It is important to understand when each change to § 2-402 went into effect because the version that will be applied to determine punishment will be the version in effect on the date the offense happened. The changes are not retroactive. This can lead to clearly unjust results. Consider the following example. Defendant gets arrested for possession of meth on June 30, 2017. It's a felony to possess it on that date. The next day, on July 1, 2017, that same offense becomes a misdemeanor. Had Defendant been arrested just the next day, he would have been charged with just a misdemeanor. Prosecutors do have the ability to charge that offense as a misdemeanor under another statute, but it is up to their discretion whether to use it.

Penalties For Possession Of A CDS Prior to November 1, 2016

The law covering simple possession that was superseded on November 1, 2016 had harsher penalties than the law that superseded it. The law that went into effect on November 1, 2016 removed some mandatory minimums and reduced some maximums.

Penalties For Possession Of A CDS In Oklahoma (November 1, 2016 - to July 1, 2017)

Possession of any Schedule I or II substance, except marijuana, is a felony, and you can spend up to five years in the Department of Corrections and pay a $5,000 fine. A second violation of that law can get you up to 10 years in the Department of Corrections and a $10,000 fine. A subsequent violation of that section involving Schedule I or II drugs, except marijuana, carries a punishment ranging from 4–15 years in the Department of Corrections and a $10,000 fine.

Possession of any Schedule III, IV, or V substance, including marijuana, is a misdemeanor for the first offense. You can spend up to one year in county jail and be fined up to $1,000.

Possession of a Schedule III, IV, or V substance, including marijuana, during the period of any court-imposed probationary term or within ten years of the date following the completion or execution of any sentence or deferred judgment and it is a second or a subsequent violation is a felony. You can spend between one to five years in the Department of Corrections and pay a fine of up to $5,000.

Possession of any CDS within 1,000 feet of a school or in the presence of a child under 12 is a felony. For a first offense, the imprisonment will be a term that is not more than twice the amount authorized by the appropriate and respective part of the statute. Also, you must serve a minimum of 50% of that sentence before you become eligible for good time credit. If you have a second or subsequent offense of possessing drugs within 1,000 feet of a school or in the presence of a child aged 12 or younger, then you must serve a minimum of 90% of your sentence before being eligible to earn good time credits. The fine can be up to $10,000.

Penalties For Possession Of A CDS In Oklahoma (Starting July 1, 2017)

The laws covering possession of a CDS in Oklahoma radically change on July 1, 2017. Starting on that date, the unlawful (simple) possession of any CDS will be a misdemeanor. The maximum time in jail will be one year, and the maximum fine will be $1,000. There will be no difference in the maximum penalty based on how many times someone has violated that statute. So, for example, someone could get caught with possession of a small amount of meth 20 times, and that individual would be charged with a misdemeanor for each of those 20 cases.

Possession in the presence of a child or near a school will no longer be taken into consideration.

SOURCES:
63 OS § 2-402 (Superseded 11/1/16)
63 OS § 2-402 (Superseded 7/1/2017)
63 OS § 2-402 (Effective 7/1/2017)

POSSESSION WITH INTENT TO DISTRIBUTE

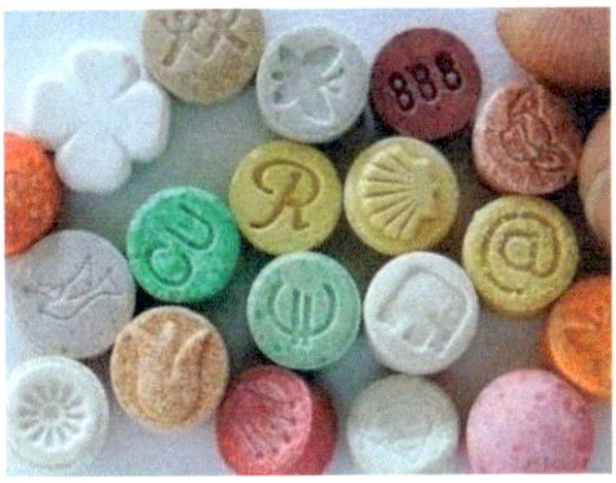

Possession with the intent to distribute (PWID) carries stricter penalties than simple possession of drugs. If you're caught with what the police believe to be a large amount of drugs and/or you are caught with drugs and paraphernalia that may make it appear as though you were engaged in the sale and distribution of drugs, then you can be charged with PWID. Even if you had a large amount of drugs that was only for personal use, you can still be charged with PWID.

Something to keep in mind for PWID is that it's *not necessarily* possession with intent to *sell*. Many people think they can only be found guilty of possession with intent to distribute if they were either caught in the act of selling or were planning on selling the drugs. That is not true. You can be found guilty of possession with intent to distribute for way less than selling drugs. The statute, among other things, says that someone violates this law if they "distribute, dispense, transport with intent to distribute or dispense, possess with intent to manufacture, distribute, or dispense, a controlled dangerous substance or to solicit the use of or use the services of a person less than eighteen (18) years of age to cultivate, distribute or dispense a controlled dangerous substance . . . ." The word "sell" is not found anywhere in the statute.

The threshold for something to constitute "intent to distribute" is actually quite low. For example, let's say you are smoking marijuana with a group of people and y'all are passing around a joint. If you have that joint in your hands and *intend to* pass it to another person after you take a hit, then you *can* be found guilty of PWID because you intended to give it to another person. And note that you don't even have to give it to someone. You just have to *intend to* give it to someone. Take another example where you are stopped by law enforcement on the road. They find drugs and question you about them. You casually say that you were merely bringing them over to a friend's house because he left them at your house the previous night. Well, you likely just talked yourself into a felony PWID charge. It doesn't matter that no money is to be exchanged or that you'd test clean for drugs. All that matters is that you intended to give those drugs to someone else.

Penalties For PWID In Oklahoma

The statute that covers PWID in Oklahoma is 63 OS § 2-401. Every charge of PWID is a felony. If it's a Schedule I or II drug that's narcotic a drug, LSD, GHB and several others, then you can be imprisoned for five years to life and fined up to $100,000. If it's any other drug that is a Schedule I, II, III or IV drug, then you can be imprisoned for two years to life and fined up to $20,000. If it's a Schedule V drug, then you can be imprisoned for up to five years and a fined up to $1,000.

What Happens When Someone Is Charged With PWID In Oklahoma After Having Been Convicted Of PWID?

Any person convicted more than once for PWID will be considered a habitual offender and sentenced under 21 OS § 51.1.

SOURCES:
63 OS § 2-401
21 OS § 51.1

DRUG TRAFFICKING

The primary factor in determining trafficking of illegal drugs is the quantity of the drug. The following table shows the quantities that constitute trafficking and the amount of fine.

Drug	Quantity	Minimum Fine	Maximum Fine
Marijuana	≥ 25 lbs.	$25,000	$100,000
Aggravated	≥ 1,000 lbs.	$100,000	$500,000
Cocaine or coca leaves	≥ 28 g.	$25,000	$100,000
	≥ 300 g.	$100,000	$500,000
Aggravated	≥ 450 g.	$100,000	$500,000
Heroin	≥ 10 g.	$25,000	$50,000
	≥ 28 g.	$50,000	$500,000
Amphetamine or Meth	≥ 20 g.	$25,000	$200,000
	≥ 200 g.	$50,000	$500,000
Aggravated	≥ 450	$50,000	$500,000
LSD	≥ 1 g.	$50,000	$100,000
	≥ 10 g.	$100,000	$250,000
PCP	≥ 20 g.	$20,000	$50,000
	≥ 150 g.	$50,000	$250,000

Cocaine Base	≥ 5 g.	$25,000	$100,000
	≥ 50 g.	$100,000	$500,000
MDMA (Ecstasy)	≥ 30 tabs or 10 g.	$25,000	$100,000
	≥ 100 tabs or 10 g.	$100,000	$500,000
Morphine	≥ 1000 g.	$100,000	$500,000
Hydrocodone	≥ 3,750 g.	$100,000	$500,000
Benzodiazepines	≥ 500 g.	$100,000	$500,000

The term of imprisonment for a first-time offense is at least twice the term of imprisonment provided for in 63 OS § 2-401. The following table shows the amount of prison time for each offense.

Drugs	First Offense	After 1 trafficking or UCDSA felony conviction	After 2 or more trafficking and / or UCDSA felony convictions	After 2 or more trafficking violations
Heroin, Cocaine, Hydrocodone, Oxycodone, Morphine, or LSD	10 years - life	15 years - life	20 years – life without parole	Life without parole
Marijuana, Amphetamine, Meth, MDMA, Benzodiazepines	4 years – life	6 years - life	20 years – life without parole	Life without parole

Aggravated trafficking marijuana, amphetamine, meth, cocaine, or coca	15 years – life. Must serve 85% before being eligible for parole consideration or earned credits.	21 OS § 51.1 applies	21 OS § 51.1 applies	Life without parole

Individuals convicted of trafficking are not eligible for deferred or suspended sentences. Any person convicted of trafficking shall, in addition to any fine imposed, pay a trauma-care fee of $100.00.

SOURCES:

63 OS § 2-415

63 OS § 2-401

21 OS § 51.1

Note to Oklahoma Legislature: Not every "drug trafficker" is Tony Montana.

POSSESSION OF A CDS WITHOUT A TAX STAMP

Because simple possession of a CDS becomes a misdemeanor on July 1, 2017, some DAs offices will use 68 OS § 450.8 to try and get a felony conviction for mere simple possession of a CDS. The law applies to someone who is a "dealer," which is defined as a person who, in violation of the Uniform Controlled Dangerous Substances Act, manufactures, distributes, produces, ships, transports, or imports into Oklahoma or in any manner acquires or possesses more than 42.5 grams of marijuana, or seven or more grams of any CDS other than marijuana, or ten or more dosage units of any CDS other than marijuana which is not sold by weight. For purposes of this law, a CDS is a drug, substance, or immediate precursor specified in Schedules I through V of the Uniform Controlled Dangerous Substances Act which is held, possessed, transported, transferred, sold or offered to be sold in violation of the laws of Oklahoma.

Any "dealer" manufacturing, distributing, producing, shipping, transporting, importing or possessing any CDS without affixing the appropriate stamp, upon conviction, is guilty of a felony punishable by imprisonment in the Department of Corrections for not more than five years or by the imposition of a fine of not more than $10,000.00, or by both such imprisonment and fine. Of course, nobody will have a tax stamp, so simple possession of a certain amount of drugs can violate this statute in addition to the one that the voters changed (63 OS § 2-402).

Since nobody is going to attempt to get a tax stamp on an illegal drug, anyone in possession of an illegal controlled dangerous substance in the above amounts can be found guilty of violating the Controlled Dangerous Substances Tax Act. This is their way of circumventing the will of the voters who voted for State Question 780 on November 8, 2016.

SOURCES:
68 OS § 450.1
68 OS § 450.8

DUI-DRUGS

DUI in Oklahoma is defined in 47 OS § 11-902 and describes the offense as someone who:

- has a blood or breath alcohol concentration that's 0.08 or more; or
- *has any amount of a Schedule I or other controlled substance or one of its metabolites or analog in their blood, saliva, urine or any other bodily fluid at the time of test*; or
- is under the influence of any intoxicating substance other than alcohol, which may render that person incapable of safely driving or operating a motor vehicle; or
- is under the combined influence of alcohol and any other intoxicating substance which may render that person incapable of safely driving or operating a motor vehicle.

Any test must be conducted within two hours of the arrest.

Note the language discussing "any amount of a Schedule I or a controlled substance or any of its metabolites or

analog in the body." That signifies that Oklahoma is a zero-tolerance state. If someone has any measurable amount of those substances in their body, then he or she is automatically considered to have been driving under the influence. This is extremely harsh!

This means that you can still be found guilty of DUI-drugs if you have *any* amount of a Schedule I drug or a controlled substance or *any* of their metabolites or analog in your body—even if you were driving perfectly fine! This can come into play when someone is pulled over, the officer asks the driver if he or she has taken any drugs, and the driver—not knowing this law—states that they consumed some substance that morning or a previous day. If the officer wanted to, they could request to take a sample of the driver's blood. If the driver refuses, then it's treated as a refusal. For license revocation purposes, there's no distinction between a refusal for DUI-drugs and an alcohol-related DUI refusal. After the revocation period, the driver will still have to place an interlock in their car even though they did not have any alcohol in their system!

Keep in mind that DPS only revokes licenses for alcohol in the system—not drugs. If blood is taken and an illegal substance (and no alcohol) is found, the license will *not* be revoked. The driver will not have to place an interlock in their car. However, test results indicating the presence of drugs will be used for the criminal prosecution.

What makes this law extra harsh is how long some people can be considered "DUI" after ingesting a drug. For instance, heavy marijuana users may have THC metabolites in their blood for up to a month after the last ingestion. Due to Oklahoma's per se law, they can still be found guilty of DUI-drugs even with no THC in their system and after having not smoked for weeks. Furthermore, the statute also makes it possible for you to be held "under the influence" if you're taking prescribed medication that you ordinarily wouldn't think would intoxicate someone, such as Prozac, so long as you were rendered incapable of safely driving or operating a motor vehicle.

If you are stopped and asked by a law enforcement officer if you've taken any drugs, it would be a good idea to not disclose any information about drug use—legal or illegal. If you do, then you could very well be talking yourself into a DUI-drugs charge. Don't give law enforcement the probable cause they need to further investigate that crime.

Note that an officer will not automatically want to get your blood if you admit to taking drugs. Decrease the officer's motivation to hit you with more charges by being polite and respectful. An officer will be more likely to throw the book at someone who is rude and combative.

SOURCES:
47 OS § 11-902
47 OS § 754
47 OS § 6-205.1

ENDEAVORING TO COMMIT A DRUG OFFENSE

Endeavoring to commit a drug offense is covered in 63 OS § 2-408. It is defined in OUJI-CR 6-16 as any effort to do or accomplish the evil purpose that the law was enacted to prevent. This is a VERY LOW standard—even lower than "attempt." It's basically any effort, no matter how slight, towards the attainment of your goal.

For example, you have drugs, and I know you have drugs. If I take one step in your direction, then I could potentially be found guilty of "endeavoring to possess drugs." Someone can be charged with endeavoring to possess drugs by merely pointing another in the direction of a drug dealer. This is a very scary statute because the threshold to violate it is so low. So, if you don't want to get charged with this offense, then don't do anything that would give law enforcement the idea that you are trying to get drugs or help someone else get drugs.

The penalty for violating this statute is the penalty for the offense you're supposedly endeavoring to commit.

SOURCES:

63 OS § 2-408

OUJI-CR 6-16

CONSPIRACY TO COMMIT A DRUG OFFENSE

Conspiracy to commit a drug offense is covered in 63 OS § 2-408. Conspiracy is defined in OUJI-CR 2-17 as 1) an agreement by two or more persons; 2) to commit a crime; 3) the defendants were parties to the agreement at the time it was made or they knowingly became parties to the agreement at some time after it was made; and 4) there was an overt act by one or more of the parties performed subsequent to the formation of the agreement.

The reason this comes up so much in drug cases is because more than one person is typically involved in the distribution of drugs. If an officer stops a car with more than one person in the car and the car has a significant amount of drugs, then chances are high that everybody in the car will be charged with conspiracy to distribute/traffic. The theory is that everyone in the car was aware of and participating in the illegal activity.

The penalty for violating this statute is the penalty for the offense you supposedly conspired with another to commit.

SOURCES:

63 OS § 2-408

OUJI-CR 2-17

STATUTE OF LIMITATIONS FOR FILING A DRUG CHARGE

The statute of limitations in Oklahoma is governed by 22 OS § 152. Drug cases fall under the general section of that statute. It states that the prosecution for the offense must be commenced within three years after its commission. Therefore, the prosecutor has three years to file charges after the commission of a drug offense.

SOURCE:
22 OS § 152

Alternative Programs Available To Drug Offenders

Most counties in Oklahoma have a drug court program. However, there are some very stringent requirements for that program.

The following are the basic requirements to enter drug court in Oklahoma:

1. The offender's arrest or charge does not involve a crime of violence against any person, unless there is a specific treatment program in the jurisdiction designed to address domestic violence and the offense is related to domestic violence and substance abuse;
2. The offender has no prior felony conviction in this state or another state for a violent offense within the last ten years, except as may be allowed in a domestic violence treatment program authorized by the drug court program.;
3. The offender's arrest or charge does not involve a violation of the Trafficking In Illegal Drugs Act;
4. The offender has committed a felony offense; and
5. The offender:
   a. admits to having a substance abuse addiction,
   b. appears to have a substance abuse addiction,

c. is known to have a substance abuse addiction,

d. the arrest or charge is based upon an offense eligible for the drug court program, or

e. is a person who has had an assessment authorized by 43A OS § 3-704 and the assessment recommends the drug court program.

Updates To Rehabilitation Programs

On November 1, 2016, drug court expanded eligibility to include persons recommended for drug court after a Mental Health and Substance Abuse Assessment and Evaluation. The change also implies that drug court need not be in lieu of incarceration. State Question 781 proposed using the money saved by enacting State Question 780 for drug rehabilitation programs. I think the public is realizing that harm to society by the incarceration of drug addicts is greater than the drugs themselves. They now realize that a higher priority should be placed on rehabilitation instead of incarceration.

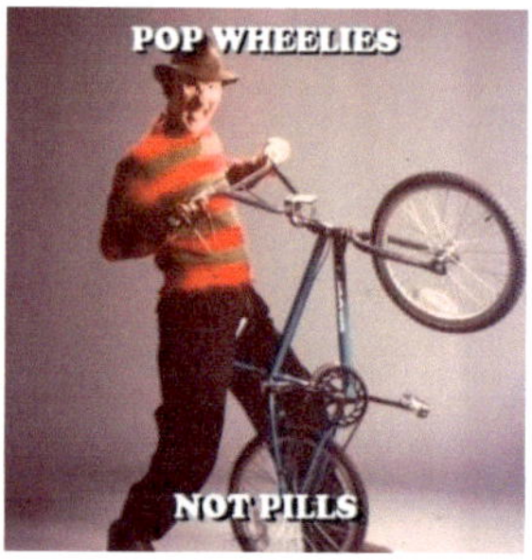

SOURCES:
63 OS § 2-402
22 OS §§ 471–472

SUBMITTING TO A SEARCH

The law governing all searches and seizures is the Fourth Amendment to the United States Constitution. It states that "the right of the people to be secure in their person, houses, papers, and effects against unreasonable searches and seizures shall not be violated, and no warrant shall issue, but upon a probable cause accorded by oath, or affirmation and particularly describing the place to be searched, and the person or thing to be seen." **You don't have to consent to a search.** In fact, it's not a good idea to ever consent to a search. However, there are many situations where the police may search your person, vehicle, or home without your consent.

The Warrant Requirement

A warrant is usually required for law enforcement to conduct a search. However, there are a variety of situations where a warrant is not required. When a warrant is issued, it may only be based on probable cause.

A warrant is required before a search or seizure, unless there are exigent circumstances. An arrest warrant is not constitutionally required. Any search, whether there is a warrant or not, must not be unreasonable. A Fourth Amendment search and seizure only takes place when a person's reasonable expectation of privacy has been violated. Nonetheless, some types of evidence are likely to be found not protected by a reasonable expectation of privacy. They are: abandoned property (e.g. trash); things that can be seen from an aerial view, or from an officer's vantage point on public property; things that a person says or does in public; and information law enforcement learns by use of other senses while they are in a place they have a right to be.

Probable Cause

Probable cause is required to make an arrest or conduct a search. Probable cause applies to two different situations: 1) before a judge or a magistrate may issue a warrant for an arrest or search and 2) before law enforcement can make a warrantless search or arrest. For there to be probable cause to arrest a person, it must be reasonably likely that a violation of the law has been committed and the person to be arrested committed the violation. For there to be probable cause to search a particular location, there must be likelihood that the specific items to be searched are connected to criminal activities and these items will be found in the place searched.

Exceptions To Search Warrants

The general rule is that a warrant is required for a search. However, the requirements for a search warrant may be dispensed with if some special exception applies. The most common exceptions are: search incident to a valid arrest, a search motivated by exigent circumstances, certain types of automobile searches, searches done after consent, "stop and frisk" partial searches, and certain inspections and regulatory searches.

In some, but not all, of these situations, the officer must have a probable cause to believe that a search will furnish evidence of the crime, even though they are not required to get a warrant. In others, something less than probable cause will be needed. This includes "stop and frisk" and a consent search.

Search Incident To Arrest

When an officer makes a lawful arrest, they may search the area in any arrestee's control. Only the area that is theoretically within the defendant's immediate control is searched incident to the arrest. There could be automobile searches incident to an arrest. In most driver arrests for traffic violations, the police aren't entitled to search the passenger compartment incident to an arrest. The basic rule on automobile searches incident to an arrest is that a warrantless search incident to an arrest must be limited in the areas within the arrestee's immediate control. If the officer reasonably believes that the passenger compartment might contain evidence of the offense for which the arrest is being made, they may search that compartment. This rationale would almost never apply to a traffic arrest, but will often apply to arrests for drug offenses. This is a very low standard.

If the officer reasonably concludes that the driver may be dangerous and might gain access to a weapon in their car once they've returned to the car post-investigation, under a form of stop and frisk, the officer may conduct a brief protective search of the passenger compartment for weapons. When law enforcement properly stops a car, whether they arrest the driver or not, if they have probable cause to believe that the vehicle contains contraband, or evidence of crimes, they may search any part of the vehicle where the evidence might plausibly be found. For example, if the officers are looking for something big like a rifle, they can't search small containers where they think drugs might be. However, if they think that the contraband is drugs, which of course may be small, then they can look in anything that might contain that evidence of that illegal activity. For the search incident to an arrest option to apply, the arrest must be a custodial one, which means that the officer must be planning to take the defendant to the station for booking.

Exigent Circumstances

There may be exigent circumstances that justify dispensing with the warrant requirements. The most common are: preventing the imminent destruction of evidence, preventing harm to a person, and hot pursuit of a suspect.

The "Plain View" Doctrine

In general, law enforcement does not commit a Fourth Amendment search when an officer sees an object that is in plain view and the officer has the right to be in the position to have that view. When an officer is using an aircraft to view a property, anything they see with the naked eye falls into the plain view doctrine as long as the aircraft is in public navigable airspace. The plain view doctrine also applies to senses other than sight, such as touch, hearing, or smell. This is how officers are able to stop and frisk alleged suspects. If an officer is conducting a legal pat down under stop and frisk, and he or she touches something that feels like contraband, the officer may seize it that under the plain touch analog to the plain view doctrine. The plain touch doctrine only applies if the officer has the right to do the touching in the first place.

The plain view doctrine allows officers who are on premises for lawful purposes to make a warrantless seizure of evidence that they may come across. For this doctrine to apply, three requirements must be met: the officer must not have violated the Fourth Amendment in arriving at the place from which the item is plainly viewed; the incriminating nature of the items must be immediately apparent; and the officers must have a lawful right of access to the object itself.

Automobile Searches

All the general exceptions also apply to automobiles. With automobiles however, it is easier for law enforcement to search them due to the automobile exceptions. The two major exceptions specific to automobiles are 1) the vehicle may be searched at the station house without a warrant when the driver is arrested (inventory exception) and 2) the vehicle may be subjected to a full warrantless search in the field if the police reasonably believe that a vehicle is carrying contraband.

When a driver is stopped and an officer wants to search the vehicle on the scene, they'll normally need probable cause to conduct a search. If an officer finds evidence in plain view of a vehicle as they are impounding it, they may seize the evidence even though they may not have previously had probable cause to search or seize. If the vehicle has been impounded by the police pursuant to standardized procedures, law enforcement may conduct a search at the station even though they don't have probable cause. This is the "inventory search." With an inventory search, law enforcement must follow standardized procedures and must not be acting in bad faith or for the sole purpose of investigation.

The inventory search is just a ruse to allow officers to search the vehicle of anybody who is arrested. So long as someone is arrested, an officer can search every inch of the vehicle. The official reason is to make sure that every item in the vehicle is accounted for, but it's really an excuse to let the officers search every nook and cranny of a vehicle.

The exception allowing law enforcement to search a vehicle because they reasonably believe that it has contraband commonly applies to drugs. The typical scenario occurs when an officer walks up to a vehicle and smells an odor of marijuana. The officer then has probable cause to search the vehicle. The bottom line is that if you don't want an officer searching your vehicle, then you should neither smoke pot in it nor carry around pot in it. Any smell of marijuana will result in a search of your vehicle in Oklahoma.

An officer may search a passenger only if the officer has probable cause to believe that the passenger possesses evidence of a crime or the officer has probable cause to arrest the passenger. The officer has several other rights regarding passengers. As a method of protecting the officer, the officer may demand the passenger step out of the vehicle. Many people don't think they have to exit the vehicle when the officer asks them to. However, in the vast majority of situations, the officer is well within his or her rights to demand someone exit the vehicle because the officer can always say that it's for officer safety. In addition, an officer may have a fear that the passenger is armed and dangerous. As a matter of protection, the officer may frisk and pat down the passenger to make sure that the passenger is not carrying any weapons. If the officer has the right to search a vehicle, the officer may also search any container in a car that may contain the object that he is looking for—even if the officer knows that the container belongs to a passenger. The officer can do this even if they have no probable cause to believe that the container contains that object!

Consent Searches

Law enforcement may make a warrantless search if they receive the consent of the individual whose premises, effects, or persons are to be searched. It boggles my mind that people who know they have drugs in their vehicle or on their person consent to a search. This happens all the time. I don't think you should consent to a search—even if you don't think you have drugs on you or in the vehicle.

I've seen situations where people didn't think they had drugs on them, however, officer finds drugs. Now they are charged with a crime.

Stop And Frisk

If an officer observes unusual conduct that leads the officer to reasonably conclude that criminal activity is afoot, the officer may briefly detain the suspect in order to make inquiries. Probable cause is not required. The officer needs only reasonable suspicion based on objective facts that the individual is involved in criminal activity. After the stop, the officer may conduct a limited search of the outer clothing of the suspect in an attempt to discover weapons.

The stop and frisk doctrine also allows an officer to stop a vehicle. The typical scenario is someone being pulled over for traffic infraction. Once the officer conducts a justified stop, the officer may require the driver and the passengers to get out of the car as a legitimate safety measure. Law enforcement is entitled to do a pat down of any passenger whom they have reasonable suspicion to believe are armed and dangerous.

Vague suspicion is not enough. The officer may stop a suspect only if he or she has reasonable suspicion based on objective facts that the suspect is involved in criminal activity. An officer cannot go on hunches. Only reasonable suspicion is required for a stop. Probable cause is required for an arrest. When law enforcement officers perform a frisk after making a stop, the frisk must be limited to a search for weapons or other sources of danger. The frisk may not be to search for contraband or incriminating evidence. However, the police may lawfully discover drugs or other contraband under the plain touch analogue to the plain view exception.

SOURCES:

Terry v. Ohio
Katz v. U.S.
Florida v. Riley
U.S. v. Watson
Atwater v. Lago Vista
Arizona v. Gant

U.S. v. Robinson
Rawlings v. Kentucky
Chambers v. Maroney
U.S. v. Ross
Calif. V. Carney
Wyoming v. Houghton
California v. Acevedo
Colorado v. Bertine
South Dakota v. Opperman
Brown v. Texas
Adams v. Williams
Pennsylvania v. Mimms
Maryland v. Wilson

CAN A PASSENGER BE CHARGED IF DRUGS ARE DISCOVERED IN THE VEHICLE?

The important principle that applies to vehicle passengers is the concept of constructive possession. There are three different types of possession: actual possession, constructive possession, and joint possession. OUJI-CR 6-11 defines these types of possession.

Actual Possession

Actual possession is the easiest to understand. This is where you have physical possession of the drugs somewhere on your person. For example, you have actual possession of drugs when the baggie is in your pocket.

Constructive Possession

Constructive possession is the most difficult concept to understand because the drugs are not on the defendant's person. For example, you have drugs in a glove compartment; they are not on your person. You know they're there and can control the disposition of them. Therefore, you have constructive possession of those drugs. Someone who has constructive possession of drugs is just as guilty as someone with actual possession.

Joint Possession

Possession is joint if two or more people share actual or constructive possession of a thing. A person may be deemed to be in joint possession of drugs that are in the physical custody of an associate if that person willfully and knowingly shares with that other person the right to control the disposition or use of the drugs. For example, a passenger may have joint possession of drugs in the driver's pocket if the passenger willfully and knowingly shared the right to control the disposition or use of those drugs.

Proximity Not Enough

A key principle to remember is that mere proximity to a substance is insufficient to prove possession. In order to prove constructive possession, an individual must have had knowledge of the items present and the power and the intent to control their disposition or use. Proof that the accused was at a place where drugs were being used or possessed is in and of itself insufficient to justify the finding of possession. There must be additional evidence of knowledge and control.

Motor Vehicle Issues

With respect to being a passenger in a motor vehicle that is not yours, you might receive a drug-related charge if the drugs are found in the car. Whether you're charged depends on a lot of factors. Where exactly were the drugs found? Were they closer to you or the other individual(s) in the vehicle? Were they in a container that only somebody else had access to (e.g. a locked glove box that only the driver had the keys to)? These are all things that an attorney is going to look for. It's important to build a case that not only did you not have actual possession but you had neither constructive nor joint possession of the drug.

SOURCE:
OUJI-CR 6-11

Getting Drug Charges Reduced Or Dismissed

It is possible to get drug charges dismissed or reduced. For first-time offenses, it's sometimes possible to work out a deal that results in nothing worse than a deferred sentence. With a deferred sentence, the defendant pleads guilty and will have some probationary requirements and time to prove that they can stay out of trouble. The charges will be dismissed once the defendant completes the requirements and they have not committed any new crimes for that period of time. They can then possibly get that case expunged from their record. But, the more charges a person has, the more difficult it makes it to get a deferred sentence.

Something I do with all my clients charged with possession of drugs is to immediately start them on classes. This begins with the ADSAC evaluation, which involves seeing a licensed counselor. They talk about the individual's use of drugs, and the counselor generally recommends a treatment regimen—usually classes. The number of class hours varies depending on the level of the type of charges or the type of drugs. Then, the individual goes back to the counselor and has a final evaluation. This helps my clients in a couple of ways. First, the client will be able to get a head start on the classes that they will likely be required to do. Second, it generally improves the plea offer from the prosecutor.

There typically must be a legal reason to have charges dismissed or reduced. A good way to get charges dismissed is to prove that the drugs belonged to somebody else. For example, if fingerprints on the bag belong to only the other person in the car, then there would be a high probability of getting that charge dismissed. A bad stop or illegal search are good reasons charges can get dismissed. If the prosecutor will have a difficult time getting that evidence admitted, then it could be possible to have the charges dropped. If I can convince a prosecutor that the client was merely present when the drugs were there and he or she had no connection to the drugs, then chances of getting charges dropped increase.

There are usually Fourth Amendment issues in drug possession cases. A lot of people who are arrested for drugs are pulled over by law enforcement or stopped by law enforcement in some way, are interrogated, and searched. Many cases are thrown out during pre-trial due to Fourth Amendment search and seizure violations. First, I need to see if the stop was legal. Officers must have reasonable suspicion to believe that there was a violation of law to pull the car over. Second, I'll look to see if the officer had probable cause to believe that the person had drugs in their car. If the stop was illegal or there was no probable cause, then there may be solid grounds for dismissal.

Even if I believed there was an illegal search, a bad stop, or my client didn't have possession, the prosecutor may still not dismiss the case because prosecutors are very reluctant to dismiss cases in general. Instead of getting charges dismissed, the plea offer may improve. It's worth it to the prosecutor for a defendant to receive a lighter punishment in order to not go through a suppression hearing and potentially lose at trial. They would rather get something instead of potentially getting nothing.

When I present these issues to the prosecutor, it's not just me telling them whatever comes to mind. I have to research these cases and the laws. I need to know my cases well and identify the issues. I find previously decided cases that have similar facts and issues of law to my cases and present them to the prosecutor. I can say, "Here's a case that was recently decided by the Court of Criminal Appeals, and they sided with the defendant. The facts of that case were similar to the facts in my case, so this is why I think you should dismiss my case."

Sometimes, a case can be dismissed due to lack of evidence. My very first case as a student public defender involved possession of marijuana. There was supposed to be a dashcam video of it. I asked repeatedly for this dashcam video. The prosecutor ultimately dismissed the case because the video that should have existed didn't exist. I made it clear that the evidence would still exist had the officer followed the correct procedure.

DEFENSE STRATEGIES USED IN DRUG-RELATED CASES

There are a variety of defense strategies that can be employed in drug-related cases. The most common are: it's not mine, illegal stop, illegal search, and not illegal drugs.

It's Not Mine

It would be helpful to show the prosecutor or the jury that the substance belonged to somebody else. Did the defendant actually possess the drug? Did the defendant have constructive or joint possession of the drug? Mere proximity to a substance is insufficient proof of possession. There must be additional evidence of the defendant's knowledge and ability to exert control over the substance. Such knowledge and control may be established by circumstantial evidence. For example, I'm standing on a sidewalk. Somebody walks by me, and they drop a bag of drugs in front of me. I don't even see them do this. The police walk up to me, and they see this bag of drugs in

front of me. Do I have possession? No way! I certainly don't have actual possession, and I don't even have constructive possession. I had no knowledge of the drugs. The mere presence of drugs in proximity to somebody is insufficient to prove that the person possessed the drugs.

Illegal Stop

Did the officer truly have reasonable suspicion to believe that a crime was committed that enabled them to stop the vehicle? For instance, if the police officer says that the reason for stopping the car was a broken taillight, then it's important to know whether the taillight was actually broken. An officer can only pull you over for a lawful reason. They can't make up reasons to pull people over. If the stop is bad—or illegal—then any evidence gained after it should be thrown out.

Illegal Search

Did the officer have probable cause to believe that a crime was committed that enabled them to conduct a search? Did one of the exceptions exist that allowed them to conduct a search? If the exception did not exist, and there was no warrant, then it was an illegal search. Anything discovered because of that search should be suppressed and not allowed to be entered into evidence.

Not Illegal Drugs

People carry around all sorts of things that law enforcement may believe are drugs. It is possible to get arrested for possessing a substance that is perfectly legal. The field test kits that officers sometimes use frequently give false positives. Some kits have given false positives for chocolate, oregano, aspirin, and even air! Test kit results should be looked at with much skepticism. The substance should be sent to the OSBI crime lab to get tested. It's also possible that mistakes at the lab can result in false report results.

SOURCE:
http://thefreethoughtproject.com/marijuana-advocacy/

WORKING AS AN INFORMANT WITH THE POLICE ON A DRUG CASE

There are some benefits to working as an informant with law enforcement. There are also major drawbacks. The biggest benefit of working as an informant is that it can improve the plea recommendation in your criminal case. Typically, people who become informants are people who were arrested and the police try to get that person to roll on others. The typical scenario with drugs is that somebody was arrested for drug possession. The police want to know who their dealer is so the police can set up a controlled buy with that dealer. Charges against an informant can go completely away, get reduced, or be modified. This all depends on the original charge and the help given to police.

There are also drawbacks to becoming an informant. The first is that you could be putting your life in danger. The people you would be informing on are probably not going to be happy that you are working with the police. They are probably dangerous people and/or have connections to dangerous people. Therefore, there are many things to take into consideration when deciding to become a confidential informant.

You can receive a good deal with your case, however, that won't mean anything if you are not around to appreciate it. If police approach you for information on criminal activity, then you should tell your attorney immediately. It will be very beneficial to have an attorney to make sure that your rights are protected. An attorney can make sure that the police keep up their end of the bargain, make sure your identity is protected, protect you from incriminating yourself in additional crimes, and help you get meaningful results. Your attorney should get the deal in writing and be present any time you talk with the police. The bottom line is that if you choose to help the police, then make sure they don't hang you out to dry.

What Sets The Urbanic Law Firm Apart In Handling Drug Cases?

You don't want somebody who handles criminal cases every now and then. The Urbanic Law Firm has handled numerous cases involving drugs ranging from possession of paraphernalia to drug trafficking.

I aggressively defend all my clients. I try to get my hands on as much evidence as possible. This includes the police report, video, audio, and witness statements. I will compare what the officer did, or said they did, to the standard procedures.

As prescription drug use increases and marijuana legalization efforts continue to succeed, there will be a greater likelihood of DUI-drug arrests. It's important for an attorney to know the procedures law enforcement must follow when arresting an individual whom they believe was driving under the influence of drugs.

Not only am I a Standard Field Sobriety Test (SFST) practitioner, but I am also a SFST instructor. I have gone through the same NHTSA-certified training that law enforcement officers go through to be eligible to teach SFSTs at the academy.

There is a certain way to administer the field sobriety tests. Many officers are not proficient in the administration of those tests, so it's crucial to have an attorney who can spot the errors. It is very powerful to a jury when the defense attorney knows more about SFSTs than the officer and can highlight the officer's lack of knowledge.

Additionally, I am an Advanced Roadside Impaired Driving Enforcement (ARIDE) practitioner. ARIDE is the DUI-drugs equivalent to SFSTs. The purpose of ARIDE is to detect someone who driving under the influence of drugs. Every officer is SFST trained, and now almost all officers are ARIDE trained. With the increasing numbers of people driving after consuming some type of "drug,"

knowing how ARIDE-trained officers operate is becoming increasingly important.

I recently completed the Drug Recognition Expert (DRE) Overview course. This course gives defense attorneys an understating of the DRE program and what it takes to become a DRE. Drug Recognition Experts are specially-trained law enforcement officers whose focus is to determine the type of drug(s) an individual is under the influence of. Their training lasts several months, and their evaluation of a suspect will typically last over an hour. ARIDE-trained officers are supposed to get probable cause for an arrest, and DREs are supposed to prove someone's intoxication beyond a reasonable doubt. An attorney who is not familiar with DRE procedures may overlook a critical error in the DRE's training records or report.

DEFINITIONS

ADSAC – Alcohol and Drug Substance Abuse Course

APC – Actual Physical Control

ARIDE – Advanced Roadside Impaired Driving Enforcement

CDS – Controlled and Dangerous Substance

DPS – Department of Public Safety

DRE – Drug Recognition Expert

DUI – Driving Under the Influence

DWI – Driving While Intoxicated

NHTSA – National Highway Transportation Safety Administration

OS – Oklahoma Statute

OSBI – Oklahoma State Bureau of Investigation

OUJI-CR – Oklahoma Uniform Jury Instruction (Criminal)

PWID – Possession With Intent to Distribute

SFST – Standard Field Sobriety Test

THC – Tetrahydrocannabinol

DISCLAIMER

This publication is intended to be informational only. No legal advice is being given, and no attorney-client relationship is intended to be created by reading this material. If you are facing legal issues, whether criminal or civil, seek professional legal counsel to get your questions answered. The law cited is current as of May 1, 2017. Laws are subject to change at any time.

THE URBANIC LAW FIRM, PLLC
1141 N Robinson Avenue
Suite 101
Oklahoma City, OK 73103
(405) 633-3420

Frank@Urbanic.Law

www.Urbanic.Law

Made in the USA
Monee, IL
05 November 2026

67385052R00057